Table of Contents

A Marble Floor for the Living Room and the Library

The atmosphere of the own home is very important to most people. Living in a cozy space does of course make people much more happy than when they have to live in a messy dump.

Luckily it's not all that difficult to create a beautiful, harmonious home which will enlighten everyone's spirits. And it doesn't have to be expensive either. As a matter of fact one can mostly use reclaimed items – whether that is furniture or even building materials.

Below you see a living room – after the new mosaic tiles have been put down.

But the place used to look very different before! However, in this book we will show you how different mosaics have been applied to floors and other things and what it looked like before and after.

PREPARATIONS

The living-room and the library used to be one big room. It was difficult to use as it had all windows on one side and a chimney and stove on the other.

It was also obvious that there were previously two rooms. It was decided to choose that option again. The room was split into a small library and a cozy living room.

However, the floor was identical in both rooms. It was a cheap imitation of wood floor made from plastic and hadn't been properly laid.

The green plastic can be seen above, which was used partly to insulate the floor below and also to level it.

First, the floor was ripped up using a crowbar. However, the materials were kept for use elsewhere. If one can reuse the materials, there is no reason not to dispose of them and pollute Mother Nature.

It was up to the homeowner to decide if the white panels at the
bottom of the wall would be removed or left in. Normally, one would
remove them but the shelves and walls were already in place.
Above, you can see the concrete floor and beige marble tiles that
were being laid. The buckets containing tile glue, which were just
mixed from 40-pound-bags purchased from the home department,
can be seen to the right. Check with your local shop to find out
which varieties are available in your area.
To save money, only one quarter of the mix was to be tile glue. The
other quarters were to consist of mortar and cement (ratio
65/35%). You can't do this everywhere. If you use too much cement,
the tiles may not be glued well enough to the floor. You can either
use the recommended materials or you can experiment to find the
best match for your needs and budget.
This cutting-corners tip won't work if you are using tiles on walls,
outside, or other surfaces. It worked in this instance. Because the
marble tiles were so heavy, gravity had to do its part.

This is one of the reasons why all of the old floor was not removed: the library shelves. As you can see on the left, some small walls (made from plaster boards) are also attached to them. So tearing everything out would have been a lot of work and would just have taken far too much time for it to be worth while.

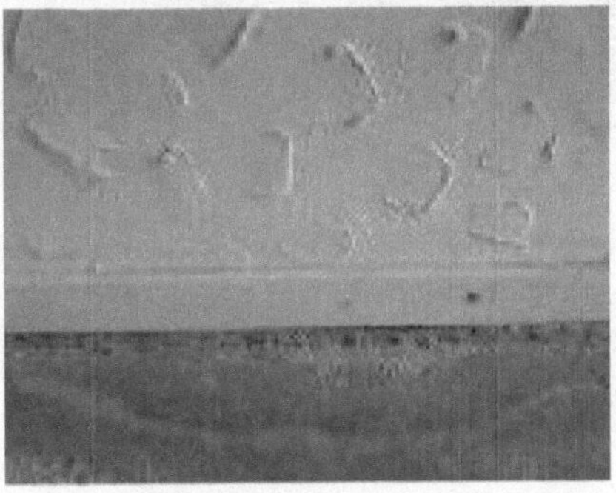

Above you can see, it is possible to work your way around that problem. One can just leave whatever is under a wall, a shelf or a panel. Later on, once the gaps between the tiles are filled out, you wouldn't be able to see anything anyway.

The same thing with the legs of the shelf in the corner. You can see everything that supports the shelf and what is beneath the panels is all still there.

Another corner of the shelf: if you take a closer look, you can see everything is still resting on the old floor.
I would however like to stress that although this is a very practical solution, this is NOT how a professional would do it!

The buckets with the tile glue – a lot of them got mixed at a time to make the work more efficient, but that also mans that one then has to hurry to get it all down while it's still soft.
Don't make it too soft though – since you wouldn't want the tiles to sink down too much.
But if the plaster is too dry and hard then it won't stick well enough to the floor either... so you have to try what works best for you and if necessary add more water as you go along.

It was up to the homeowner to decide if the white panels at the bottom of the wall would be removed or left in. Normally, one would remove them but the shelves and walls were already in place.
Above, you can see the concrete floor and beige marble tiles that were being laid. The buckets containing tile glue, which were just mixed from 40-pound-bags purchased from the home department, can be seen to the right. Check with your local shop to find out which varieties are available in your area.
To save money, only one quarter of the mix was to be tile glue. The other quarters were to consist of mortar and cement (ratio 65/35%). You can't do this everywhere. If you use too much cement, the tiles may not be glued well enough to the floor. You can either use the recommended materials or you can experiment to find the best match for your needs and budget.
This cutting-corners tip won't work if you are using tiles on walls, outside, or other surfaces. It worked in this instance. Because the marble tiles were so heavy, gravity had to do its part.

The tile glue is still wet so the floor can be finished. The tile glue is still damp so you cannot just fill in the gaps. It is best to wait until the next morning before you start filling in the gaps.
However, progress is rapid. The tiles were laid the first day. On the second day, plaster is applied to fill in the gaps. All excess filler is removed. Tiles are washed gently. Finally, the floor is cleaned thoroughly on the third day.

It takes 3 days to complete a whole room's floor. It's not easy work so it may take you longer.

Close-up of the tiles. Although the pattern looks random, it is carefully chosen so that it appears natural and fills in all the gaps. All tiles are reclaimed materials, regardless of whether they're marble, granite, or regular tiles. These tiles were originally taken from houses that had been demolished or people who just needed a new floor, a new kitchen or bathroom and called a builder.
The builder must pay for the delivery of his tile-rubber to the dump or for the removal of a container. You can ask if you can get them free of charge. Often, they will gladly give them away as it saves both time and money.
All the stones and tiles are actually garbage (garbage). They were thrown away as they are often broken and covered in old plaster. But that can be removed.

Entrances can be a challenge. This is a terrace door, so naturally you want to make sure that the edges are smooth once the gaps are all filled out and that the tiles aren't too high or too low. Everything needs to look harmonious and you also have to make sure that the rain won't gather in an unfortunate place.

Here we have another challenge. One room is about to be finished, while the other one has still the old floor in.
The floor was done in two steps, just so it wouldn't be too overwhelming and so one wouldn't have to find a place to store the furniture of two rooms at the same time.

DAY 2

You can see above a spatula that is quite large. You can get it in
different seizes. It measures approximately 35 cm in length.
After filling the gaps between tiles with a special plaster mixture
(filler), it is time to remove any excess plaster. This tool is great for
that purpose.
The rest can be wiped off with a damp sponge.
Concerning the filler-mixture, it is best to visit your local
department and ask them what they recommend. This will cost you a
lot.
You can also purchase the 50-pound bags of plaster that are used to
plaster brick houses' exterior walls and add some cement. It is
necessary to add cement to the mortar, but not too much. Otherwise
it will dry very quickly and be difficult to remove.
Alternately, you can add too much sand to the floor and it might not
seal properly. It will continue to lose sand.
It is possible to get a good result by adding 20% cement. This is a
great alternative but it doesn't offer the same results as purchasing
the correct mixture.

You can see here, in the daylight picture above, what it looks like when some of the remaining plaster is still wet and what it looks like when it's already dry.

An ordinary mop can eventually be used to wet the entire floor.

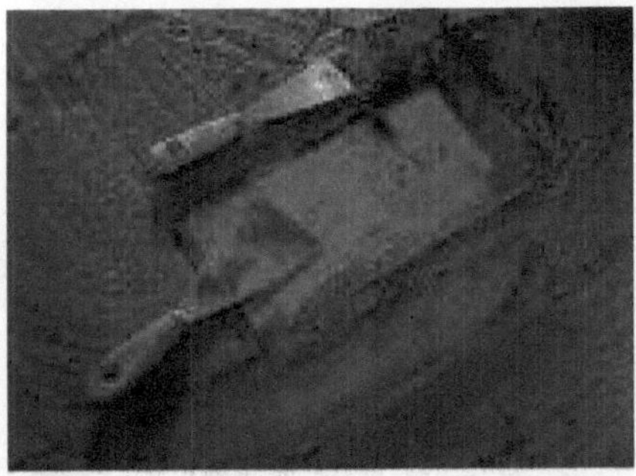

Then, you can use an ordinary spatula to remove any plaster remaining. There is still quite a bit of plaster. There are many more elegant ways to do it, and a professional builder will be able to show you these.

They are also very present at work, which I have seen. They take a lot more care and time. They spend a lot more time (and care!) on such a floor, and they then do everything perfectly. They are getting paid for their time. We don't have the time to do that. That is why we need an efficient and quick solution so we can continue with our lives.

Each solution is not perfect, and each one has pros and cons. You might be able to achieve a better result by trying different approaches.

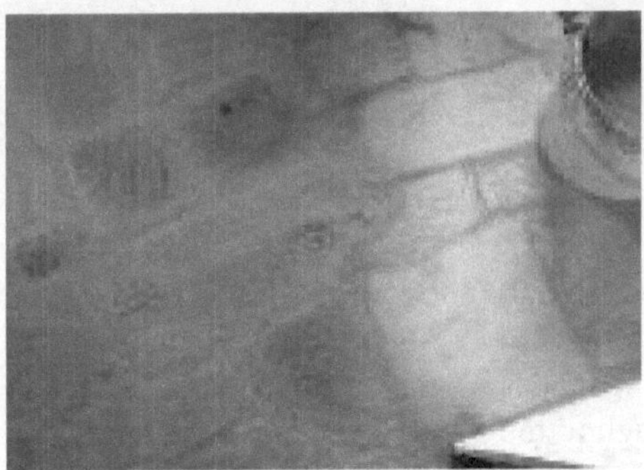

To the right we have a floor which has only been washed, not scraped. The left floor has neither been scraped, nor washed.

But even the washed side of the floor isn't good enough. It needs to be wet, scraped and washed again before it will look beautiful.

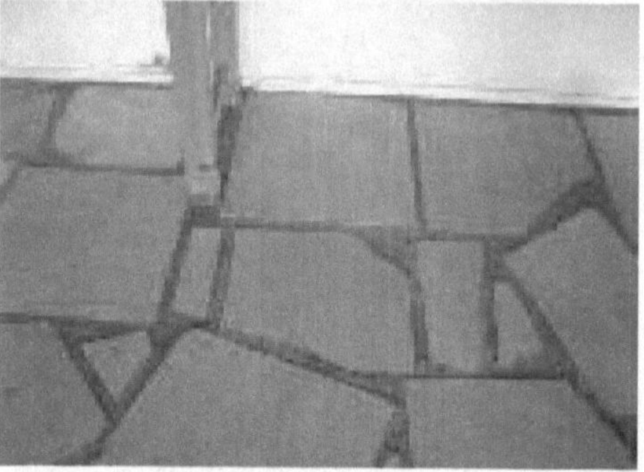

The floor beneath the library shelves: it really can't be seen that the old floor has not been removed completely. Once the panels and the wall are cleaned, everything is just going to look fine.

Above one can see a part of the floor which didn't receive enough plaster. Naturally one needs to put a little more soft plaster into the gaps between the tiles. But this doesn't always work out well enough. For one thing you don't want different shades of gray... plus the plaster needs to be able to connect well enough to the lower layer. So make sure what is already there is wet enough. You really wouldn't want anything to break off later on.

This is a neat example: everything looks pretty even and level.

Yet again this is a very personal choice: Do you want a floor which is completely level or would you like a more rustic look? The decision depends on what what your property looks like – and of course it's a matter of taste as well.

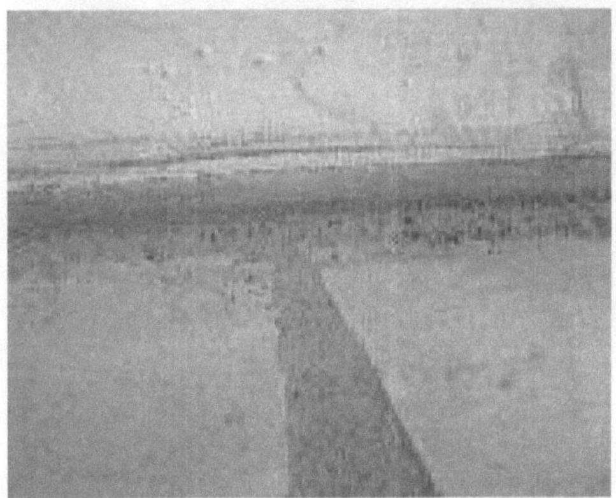

It is possible to leave the old panels in without the result looking too weird. Once everything has been cleaned and the is wall painted white again, it will look fine.

The floors took just 3 days per room, but of course all the furniture had to remove d and put back afterwards.

This is part of the library floor (at Christmas).

Here you can see how the living-room floor goes on into the library. Both have the same floor and it's a harmonious match with the rest of the interior design.

The Utility Room

Utility rooms can come with all kinds of challenges and there are in fact many different types of them.

The room featured below is a room in which both the sauna and a kiln are located. There is also a space to prepare and to dry the china; and yet the room is not very large at all..

This picture shows everything under construction. Except for the sauna, which is already done.

If you wish to see how it was built, it is featured in this book:

www.amazon.com/dp/B00VGZEAIG

The room presented a few additional challenges. The floor was not even. The floor had a large concrete block that couldn't be removed. It was the old heating system (furnace), but as a kiln is required (that's the circular thing in the first photo of this chapter, which is still wrapped up), the concrete block proved to be ideal to raise it.

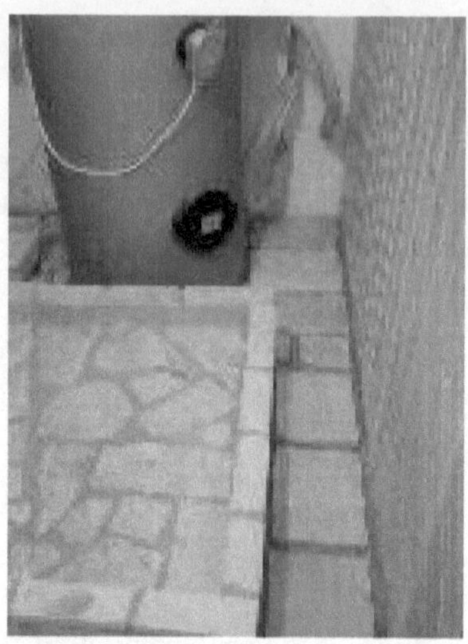

To make it look acceptable it was covered with marble mosaic tiles. The gaps of the elevated area are already filled in. The floor around it however still needs some plaster (filler).

It was to hold expensive machinery, with tiny wheels under, and it was to be used as a platform for other equipment. To ensure that the machine didn't roll off accidentally, an edge was constructed around it.
This was easy because you just had to cut the marble tiles and then put them together with lots of plaster between.

It was easy to make mini-walls, and it looked great. An edge is also created from the same marble tiles.

The gaps between the tiles are now filled out and everything is smooth and level.

Another pretty nutty challenge: Next to the electrical connections was a water tap. No sink, no nothing, just the tap!

In order to make this a little less dangerous to work with, the sockets were separated from the water installations by first of all hiding the wires behind a large marble tile.

Then a sink was built around it - from the same marble tiles that we were used elsewhere in the room, and eventually everything was this much separated, that one could no longer get harmed.

Building a sink can actually be quite easy. One just has to make sure that everything is solid and that it's watertight.

This is the final result. Although this is not a sink one would use to wash their hands, it's enough to provide water and prevent electrocution.
If you are considering applying the same solution to your home, consult an electrician first. Make sure to follow all the regulations and standards in your country.

This by the way is a trowel which is very easy to use when working with all kinds of plaster. It's very handy and not too heavy.

A final picture of the utility-room. The kiln is already in place, but the shelf in the back isn't completely finished yet. Once it's all done, it will hold the pottery that needs to dry.

This is another example of a utility-room mosaic. Made on a large and solid old frame (from a recycled painting, on a wooden surface), it now serves as the surface of a small table. For this purpose very small tile-pieces have been used.

Another utility room floor is in progress! Ordinary tiles are being used this time, as they are easy to find and are not expensive (especially if they are all broken and in a container). It makes a beautiful floor and is very easy to maintain.

These mosaic floors are made of large stones or tiles and are easy to maintain. Because they don't get as dirty as regular tile floors, you don't have to sweep them up as often as with normal tiles. They are also less slippery because they are smaller and have a rougher surface.

Here you can see both a utility-room floor and the sink which has also been surrounded by a simple gray and black mosaic surface. This is a very quick and cost-efficient way of building a working space - either for a utility room or for a kitchen.

This is a close-up of the sink. An inexpensive wooden surface was used for it. Without priming it first tile glue was applied to it and then the tiles were put on it.
One needs to however wait a day until it's properly dried.
After that the gaps were filled out, as described in the living room-chapter.

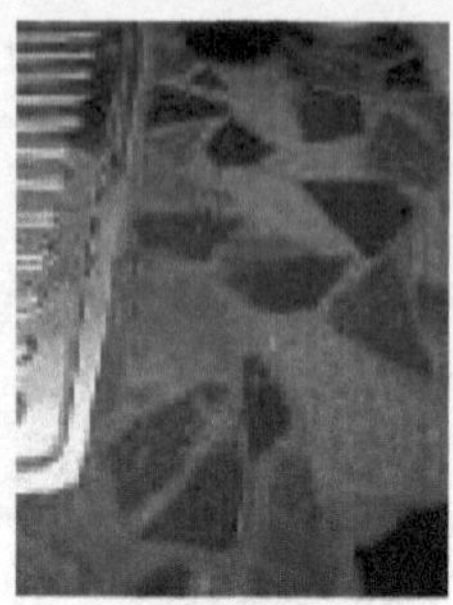

Another close-up of this sink. It is best to use the correct materials for this purpose. You won't get the right results if you mix your own grout or glue. The shop will have the most expensive stuff, but it is a smaller area than the floor, so the cost won't go up. Even if you buy the best quality, it's still affordable and much more affordable than buying cabinets or kitchen appliances for your utility room.

Granite Mosaic in the Dining Room

The old dining room was once very elegant. Although it has beautiful murals that have been updated recently, the floor was made of 150-year-old rotten hardwood, which had also been stained by fire. It was impossible to save it.

This meant one had to dig further, get rid of all the trash that was thought to be insulation, and then dig even deeper to remove soil to make room for a concrete floor with insulation.

There are many ways to insulate such a floor.

It was decided to use Leca-pearls, which are made from burned clay. They are solid and have a diameter of approximately 1 to 2 cm. This floor's bottom layer is made of Leca pearls, and concrete has Leca pearls added to it.

This is a shortcut to saving time and money. It is not the right way to do it. It turned out to be very pleasant. It is now solider and more comfortable than ever.

This is actually stage 2, because the concrete has already been filled in and as one can see the floor is pretty rough. This is due to us mixing the "Leca"-pearls into the concrete.

Now the piano. This is one of the reasons the floor was done in several stages. The piano and the stove are extremely heavy, so they were just moved within the room and not taken out like the furniture.

The other side of the room. The stove has been removed and the pipe is covered up. One can just about see the different stages in which the floor was done.

The beginning has been made and it's right in the middle of the room, beneath the chandelier.

In order to get a pretty mosaic pattern the broken granite stones get divided by their colors. The floor may look black, but a closer look reveals that both the center and the pattern around the edges (where the floor meets the walls) are actually multicolored and made from 2 different types of blue, dark green and dark red granite-stone. The rest is made from different shades of gray and black granite.

A close-up on the "center piece" of the room.

The floor has finally been put down and is getting cleaned.

Underneath the fireplace (stove) there is also a nice pattern which makes the room look special.

Here you can see how the area of the fireplace is done with much smaller stones than the rest of the floor. This is also what the granite looks like once the floor has been washed. Now the stove just needs to be put back into the area.

The final result.
It's Christmas time once again. The floor is now finished and turned out to be a very large mosaic stone floor with large gaps in between. This matched the rough and old-fashioned look this home already had.

Sharp Edges

Granite tiles, as well as all tiles, have sharp edges. You can break many small or large tiles. You can injure your self if you break the tiles.

Protect your body with appropriate clothing and be careful around your eyes. These pieces can cause serious eye injuries and even blindness. Wear protective gear and eye protection designed for this purpose. You should also remember that ordinary glasses can break.

To protect their hands, gloves are a must-have for most people.

We found that sharp edges don't have any practical value. Because you are supposed fill in the spaces between tiles, the plaster/tile filler will ensure that there are no sharp edges visible or felt when you walk on them.

This all depends on how good you do your job.

Sometimes edges can even be a benefit, as they make a floor less slippery.

A tile cutter is the best option if you don't want any sharp edges.

Marble is the material that breaks easily and leaves no sharp edges, according to my experience. Marble can even crack. We have always found it very effective to throw the tiles to make them break in a harmonious manner.

A disc grinder can also be used to cut harder stones. Protect your eyes and your entire body. Also, be aware of the dangers in your environment and ensure that sparks are not set on fire.

Although you may already know the basics, this book is widely available around the globe. I have to write them in order to ensure that no one gets hurt.

This video is about mosaic materials.

www.youtube.com/watch?v=8Z3N7mcqPFE

Youtube has many more videos about mosaic topics that should provide you with lots of inspiration.

This video is about glass-mosaic as a counter-top.

www.youtube.com/watch?v=pWERwaWLMaQ

The last video is about mosaics made with recycled materials.

This barn was converted to a shop-area with multiple use. Naturally this was a big project thus the costs had to be kept down.
Reclaimed materials were also here the solution and eventually the space looked like this:

This was quite a big project which was done in several stages which you can see in the following pictures.

First the concrete floor was leveled and all the broken areas were repaired. Then tile mosaic-floors we put in, one area at a time.

This is what it looks like when a part of the floor is done.
The procedure is always the same (as described in the chapter about the living room-floor).

Here we can see the floor, after the gaps have been filled out, but were not yet scraped and washed.

And here we have the finished floor.
The idea was to create a floor that is timeless, but still alive.

It should be neutral enough to match a Nordic style, yet it should also have a certain southern glow, in order not to look too minimalist or too sterile for an old barn.

In these last two pictures you can see two other areas of the shop. The tiles aren't too big, but also not so small as you would normally expect them to be in conventional mosaic floors.

To give everything a very rustic look, shelves were added that were made from old building materials and thin slate bars.

Pebble Walls

It is also possible to use pebbles or tile-mosaic to decorate walls. In this chapter we will show you how artist Linda Allen did her own kitchen. The walls were done many years ago and are still intact today.

Photo: Linda Allen

Here comes Linda's story:

"The pebble kitchen was started on a weekend when my husband was gone hunting. He was rather surprised when he got home, but after I received so many compliments, he started to like it a lot. It took quite a bit of time, but it was a fun project to do, since it didn't make a mess of the place and I could just work on it whenever I had the time."

Photo: Linda Allen

"I got both the pebbles and the glue at a local hobby store. In the USA you can purchase something called "mastic". It was mixed thick (like putty) and
ready to use. I liked the convenience and was willing to pay for it. Lucky for me it wasn't very expensive."
Putty:
en.wikipedia.org/wiki/Putty
The difference between mastic and putty:
www.thenakedscientists.com/forum/index.php?topic=20825.0

Pictures:
www.google.com/search?q=mastic+putty&tbm=isch
Supplier-homepage:
www.aliexpress.com/popular/mastic-putty.html

Photo: Linda Allen

"The reason I bought the rocks (pebbles) in a bag instead of at a rock quarry or Home Depot, is because they were nicely polished and somewhat consistent in shape and size. And color coordinated! I wanted the various shades of blacks & browns that buying them in a bag provided. YES, it took way over a hundred bags! I really don't know how many... but I enjoyed doing it and considered it a relaxing activity.

I have to admit, also don't like using that "mix-yourself tile glue". The "mastic" was so much easier to use. But of course you can use tile glue as well, if you prefer that."

Photo: Linda Allen

"After I was done with the kitchen, I decided to do the skylight as well. Strictly speaking it wasn't really necessary, but I wanted to give it a try, just to see what it was going to look like and luckily everyone in the family was pleased with the result."

Natural Mosaic Stone Walls

One can also decorate a wall with stones instead of rocks or pebbles. You can even use very large stones if you want to. You could even use very large slate-pieces. But since these stones are very heavy indeed, you have to make sure that not only the paste (tile glue) you use dries very quickly, you also have to hold the stones in place with big nails.

Photo: Linda Allen

The wall you see above was built from stones Linda and her family discovered in special places while on holiday. It is, so to speak, a pleasant reminder of all the great times they shared. The "mastic", which she used to build the wall, had to be kept in place for around 20 seconds to prevent them from sliding. The stones held together like glue once the "Mastic' was in place.

You will need to use regular tile glue if you are using large stones, such as large slate pieces. These stones are very heavy and you will only be able to complete one row at once while another person holds them in place. This is not an easy task. This is not an easy job.

You should be aware that slate is very hardy and can break easily when it's thrown on the floor. You will often end up with flakes rather than a clean cut. These "flakes" can easily injure someone so be cautious. We used a grinder cutter sometimes, but it was not that much more efficient or easier to cut. I like slate. It is easy to work with, and it looks timeless no matter what you do.

To cut through slate, we sometimes use a regular handsaw. Although it can be difficult, it is quite reliable.

The handsaw loses its ability to cut through wood. It won't be possible to use the handsaw on many slates before it breaks.

Patterns, Mosaic Pictures and Different Applications

I know mosaic pictures appear difficult to do, but they aren't really. The most difficult part I found was cutting the tiles, because that part of the job is just really, really boring. And depending on how thick the tiles are, it may also not be very easy to get small enough peaces.

However, when it comes to patterns, especially like the one above, this is very, very difficult to do. As you can see the marble pieces are cut precisely. This is definitely nothing for a beginner can do.

I have included this picture and the one below just for inspiration.

If I was to do a pattern like this, I would make it from small mosaic pieces or pebbles. This way it would all of a sudden become manageable – also for a beginner.

Both pictures were taken in Florence, Italy. The beautiful patterns on the outside of the cathedral are made from marble as well.

I wanted you to get inspiration both from ancient and from new mosaics, so you can come up with your own designs.
We went all over Europe to take the pictures for this chapter. Whenever we saw a mosaic that was either very simple or very beautiful, we took a picture, so we could show you in how many different ways they are applied.

The following pictures are from southern Italy. The picture above is an ancient floor, and yet it is so well preserved after hundreds of years! It looks like a real picture, but in fact it's made from tiny little tile-mosaic-pieces like you can see them on the picture below.

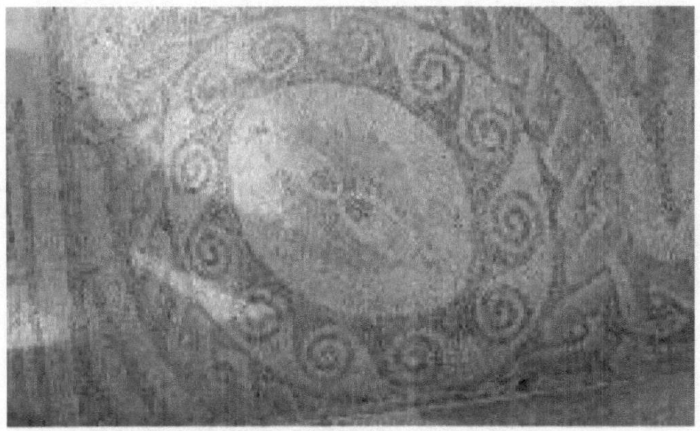

We chose this floor-pattern for the book, because this is something you can do yourself, if you like. Just practice drawing the pattern on a piece of paper. Maybe you even want to simplify it a little bit, so it becomes easier to do and then go ahead. Cut the tiles into tiny pieces (or use pebbles) and apply them to the floor, making sure you have already covered it with a layer of tile glue that is not too thick.

This is another type of pattern, which is suitable for beginners as well. But remember, if you find a pattern too difficult to do, you can always simplify it or just come up with your own pattern instead, which is inspired by old works.

This (picture above) is perhaps one of the simplest pattern I found. However it only appears to be simple, since the middle of the pattern is missing and without the picture it really does look very simple. But again this is a great opportunity to create your own designs and combine them.

Above you can see a pattern which isn't in such a good shape anymore, mainly also because the roof of the building had been missing and before it was rebuilt, this ruin had been an archaeological site like so many.

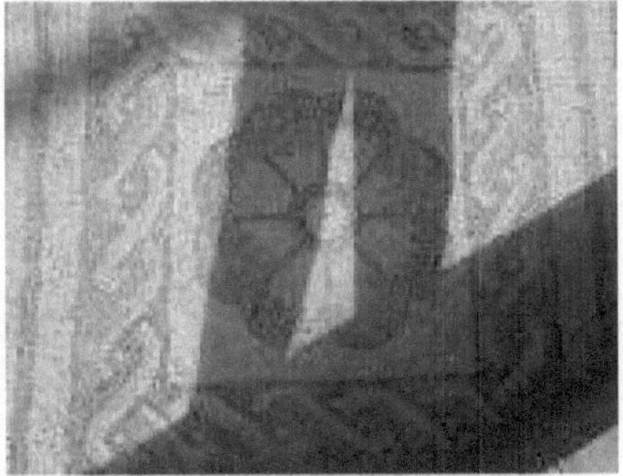

Above you can see yet another simple pattern, which would be suitable to try out for beginners. It's as Roman as it gets!

Here we have a very good example of how old simple patterns have been combined with more advanced patterns, pictures and designs.

This amazing picture is also a floor in Italy.
But you can even find ancient Roman designs in Britain.
en.wikipedia.org/wiki/Roman_mosaic

If you are looking for places to visit which have extraordinary mosaics,
"Villa Romana del Casdale" on Sicily and Hinton St. Mary
en.wikipedia.org/wiki/Hinton_St_Mary
are very special places to see.
en.wikipedia.org/wiki/Villa_Romana_del_Casale
en.wikipedia.org/wiki/Hinton_St_Mary_Mosaic

Here we have a very simple type of tile-mosaic. It takes no particular skill to do these walls and basins. This is by the way a fish-shop and the owner, an elderly gentleman, was very proud of his place, so he invited us inside to take photographs.

These tiles can be cut in half with a tile cutter. This allows you to create straight lines and 90-degree edges.
Here are photos of various tile cutters:
www.google.com/search?q=tile+cutter&tbm=isch
This is a brief, but informative Wiki-entry.
en.wikipedia.org/wiki/Ceramic_tile_cutter
This is an example youtube-video that demonstrates how it works:
www.youtube.com/watch?v=ks-gguXekmk
You can also find many other videos there.

You can either throw the tiles on to the floor or use a smaller tool for nipping pieces. To break them, you can throw them. You can also use a hammer to break them. These pieces can fly around and cause injury.

You can see the different hand tile cutters here:

www.google.com/search?q=hand+tile+cutter&tbm=isch

These videos will show you how to make mosaic with them.

www.youtube.com/watch?v=7_FbhHs-Q10

And

www.youtube.com/watch?v=D6A3iINmhOE

Youtube has many tutorials and videos that will help you understand how it all works.

Now that you know what tools you can use, you can start with simple images like these. These are easy to do and kids will have a blast with them. Everyone loves to work with colors. It just makes the time go by so much faster when you can be creative.

I found both of these pictures by the Côte d'Azur, (Port Grimaud to be precise). They were outside these little terraced houses and made the entrance look colorful and pretty.

You can see pictures of Port Grimaud here:

www.google.com/search?q=port+grimaud&tbm=isch

Wiki-Info:
en.wikipedia.org/wiki/Port_Grimaud

The picture below is from the South of France as well. I can't remember if it was a shop or a restaurant. What fascinated me, was that one can mixed both marble and pebbles. This gave a look which was both elegant and rustic at the same time.

Below you see a pattern from a hotel in northern Germany. If you want to do a pattern like this, you will have to cut the tiles precisely. Or you use pebbles or small mosaic pieces instead.

The floor below is from a mini-mall in the mountains in southern Italy. I was quite surprised, not only to find a small mall in this lonely village in the middle of nowhere, but it also surprised me how shiny and elegant the floor was. Again, if you want to do a pattern like this, use a tile-cutter to cut the pieces precisely. Or alternatively use pebbles or small tile-mosaic-pieces.

Now that we have covered different types of floors, I would like to show you what else one can do with natural stones.
Below you see a garden wall. These walls are often used to separate

different levels of a garden. Sometimes plaster is used to hold everything together,
sometimes they only use soil and small stone-pieces to make sure that nothing slides apart. The wall below was also found in Italy.

The next wall and stairs are from Sicily. It's not rocket science to build a wall like this and yet it's a timeless classic, natural and just beautiful. What is so special about this wall (and the stairs next to it) is that both are built from lava-stone. Everything is held together with a little bit of plaster.
Naturally you can find lava close to the volcano Etna, but also on some of the beaches.

Natural stones like these can also be used to build a lovely fence and a representative entrance for your property. Typically the stones are found on the grounds or close by.

The next two pictures are also from Sicily. The color of the stones is perfect and the shades mingle in, as part of the landscape. A fence like this isn't difficult to copy, if you have the materials and the time to do it.
Please remember if you live in a country where you can expect snow in

winter, you need to put a 90-cm concrete-foundation beneath such garden walls.
Unless of course your garden wall is made of two walls with soil in the middle, the sort of church walls they used centuries ago.
Any other outside wall needs both a foundation and a finishing on top. This could be tiles or simply a smooth layer of filler, which is suited for the climate. Also make sure that the sides of the falls are filled in as well and in such a manner that snow and ice won't be able to break the wall apart.

Last, not least some links which should give you many more and also very different ideas of what you can do with mosaic:
Bathroom:
naturalhomes.org/timeline/permalot-bathroom.htm
Natural homes:
naturalhomes.org/natural-
building-1.htm
en.wikipedia.org/wiki/Earths
hip
Tutorial:
kimgrantmosaics.wordpress.com/2007/08/15/how-to-make-mosaics-a-
beginners-guide
Photos:
www.google.com/search?q=mosaic+in+natural+homes&tbm=isch
You could make your own mosaic-wooden tile:
www.naturalmosaictiles.com

Museum, Chile:
www.mosaicartnow.com/2012/08/a-natural-history-museum-in-mosaic-rises-in-chile-isidora-paz-lopez
Cody Lundin:
_www.codylundin.com/codys_house.html_
Photos:
mosaik.wordpress.com/category/mosaics-around-the-world/central-and-south-america/page/2 mosaik.wordpress.com kimgrantmosaics.wordpress.
com
jeffreygardens.blogspot.dk
www.amusingplanet.com/2011/12/world-largest-coffee-bean-mosaic.html
_www.tworvgypsies.us/!USA-trip-6-2013/2013-13cd-Old_Town.html www.muralmosaic.com/usa.html_

I hope, you have enjoyed our little guide and have found some inspiration for your own interior design adventures! It is really so easy to do that anyone can try it out. Have fun!

Appendix

Text, editing and cover: M.W. James Hjortlund-
Grøndahl Co-author and credited pictures: Linda Allen
All other pictures: New Visions Publications Stock Pictures

A holiday that changes everything

On her 50th birthday everything changes. The kids are now grown up and have moved out, her husband has asked for a divorce and even her career and financial survival are endangered, due to the global financial crisis. All she's left with is doubt and regret. But then she finds a new friend who adds a new perspective to life. Sadly, life seems to hold more bad surprises in store, and all too soon that friend is taken away from her again. What is she left with now? **An unexpected vacation in Vancouver turns all that around.** All of a sudden she is able to see things for what they really are and understand why life has changed the way it did. Most of all, she can now see that her future is going to be bright. She realizes just how easily she can get what she really wants in life! This **feel-good novel** has been compared to the Meg Ryan- Comedy "French Kiss" and with **40 recipes** and more than **250 photographs of Vancouver** and many a delicacy, it is also a travel guide and a cookbook - mainly featuring delicious cakes and other baked goodies.

www.amazon.com/dp/B00CNV94ZG

Scandinavian sauna culture is known all over the world and considered a luxurious experience, close to nature. Yet building a sauna neither has to be

expensive, nor time-consuming. In fact you don't even need a lot of space nor much experience.

This is the story of how a normal family built their own sauna - completely from scratch, and with a very low budget. Illustrated with many photographs and 2 drawings this book is a **step-by-step DIY-adventure** which explains how we did it, and made the dream of our own indoor-sauna come true!

www.amazon.com/dp/B00VGZEAIG

Top Ranking on Google – for Beginners!
Find out just how easy it is to kick off your very own successful marketing campaign - without having to invest a dime! This is a **not** theoretical book.

It shows how one of the authors got his own business **on Google's first page** - FOUR TIMES, and ahead of 5,620 other search results - almost for free. B.A. Alvaang shares his secrets openly and shows you exactly how YOU can do the same! Carolyn Fawcett offers advice on **content marketing, social media, guest posting, blogs** and most of all: lots and lots of **links** which will show you where to look for all the relevant stuff that will teach you all you need to know for the future. **This simple guide can be used by anyone, anywhere.** No prerequisites are necessary.
www.amazon.com/dp/B008PYCP88

Forget New Year's Resolutions – Just Follow Your Dreams!
What do you do when New Year's resolutions lack resolve? When your plans never come to anything?
How do you get success in
life? What does it take to be
happy?
This concise, but very different, booklet on "positive thinking" and much more shows you the surest road to achieving what you want in life.
You *can* have it all: all you've dreamed of and everything that makes you happy!
But beware: this is not a book for the lazy dreamer.
It's for the ambitious dreamer who wants to make real changes in life. This booklet shares the secrets and exact steps which will get you there.
Whether you have big dreams, want to save the world or just yourself.
Whether you're looking for answers in life or just want a little more depth and peace of mind, this booklet is for you!
www.amazon.com/dp/B00HORWR3A